GENETIC ENGINEERING

SCIENCE · TECHNOLOGY · ENGINEERING

BY MICHAEL BURGAN

CHILDREN'S PRESS®

An Imprint of Scholastic Inc.

CONTENT CONSULTANT
Michael White, PhD, Assistant Professor, Washington University School of Medicine

LIBRARY OF CONGRESS CATALOGING-IN-PUBLICATION DATA
Burgan, Michael, author.
 Genetic engineering : science, technology, and engineering / by Michael Burgan.
   pages cm. — (Calling all innovators : a career for you)
 Includes bibliographical references and index.
 ISBN 978-0-531-23001-5 (library binding) — ISBN 978-0-531-23219-4 (pbk.)
 1. Genetic engineering—Vocational guidance—Juvenile literature. 2. Biotechnology—Vocational guidance—Juvenile literature. I. Title. II. Series: Calling all innovators.
 QH442.B87 2015
 660.65—dc23   2015023032

All rights reserved. Published in 2016 by Children's Press, an imprint of Scholastic Inc.
Printed in the United States of America 113

1 2 3 4 5 6 7 8 9 10 R 25 24 23 22 21 20 19 18 17 16

cience, technology, engineering, the arts, and math are the fields that drive innovation. Whether they are finding ways to make our lives easier or developing the latest entertainment, the people who work in these fields are changing the world for the better. Do you have what it takes to join the ranks of today's greatest innovators? Read on to discover if a career in the exciting world of genetic engineering is for you.

TABLE *of* CONTENTS

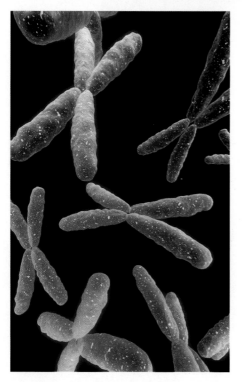

Genetic information is carried in structures called chromosomes.

Finding new fuel sources is one of the many aims of genetic engineering.

A scientist observes genetically modified tomato plants in a lab.

Genetic scientists often work with mice and other animals.

GloFish can brighten an
aquarium with their neon colors.

CHAPTER ONE

A SCIENCE OF LIFE

Looking for a colorful pet? You might want to consider GloFish. These fish glow in bright colors when they are exposed to blue light. GloFish are the product of genetic engineering, the process by which genes are altered.

All living **organisms** contain parts called **genes**. Genes determine how an organism looks and acts. Most genetic engineering involves altering genes to give an organism a new trait. Sometimes this involves making changes to an organism's natural genes. Other times it relies on blending genes from different organisms. To create the first GloFish, scientists took from a jellyfish a gene that makes the animal turn green under a blue light. They then put the gene into a zebra fish **embryo**. When it was born, the modified zebra fish had the ability to turn green, too. Different genes from other colorful sea creatures helped create the six varieties of GloFish available today.

BREAKTHROUGH DISCOVERIES

1865	1910	1953	1973
Gregor Mendel's findings about the breeding of pea plants become the foundation of genetics.	T. H. Morgan shows that **chromosomes** carry an organism's genes.	James Watson and Francis Crick create the model for the shape of **DNA**.	Stanley Cohen and Herbert Boyer show that altered DNA is passed on to future generations of a genetically modified organism.

BENEFITING FROM BIOTECHNOLOGY

For thousands of years, humans have tried to change the plants and animals around them. They usually did this to make life better for themselves. Often, they were seeking a crop that would grow faster or an animal that would produce more meat. These kinds of innovations are all types of biotechnology. Genetic engineering is a modern form of biotechnology that involves changing an organism's traits by changing its genes.

Even before humans discovered genes, they knew about **heredity**. Organisms pass on their genes when they reproduce. The next generation of the organism then has traits similar to those of its parents. This is why you might look a lot like your parents. Brothers and sisters often look alike, too, because they inherit the same genes from their parents.

Genes are the reason family members tend to look alike.

Gregor Mendel's groundbreaking studies of pea plants formed the basis of all later genetic research.

PEA PLANT

THE BEGINNING OF GENETICS

The science of genes and how they work is called genetics. Its roots go back to the work of an Austrian monk named Gregor Mendel. During the 1860s, Mendel bred peas that produced different colored seeds. He tracked the color of the seeds each generation produced. Mendel set down laws that described the odds of a plant "child" getting certain traits. But he didn't know that genes were part of the process.

During the last decades of the 19th century, many scientists studied the cells inside living organisms. The human body is made up of trillions of these microscopic units. Some organisms are so small that they consist of just a single cell.

The center of a cell is called the nucleus. Studying cells under microscopes, scientists discovered in the nucleus structures they called chromosomes. In 1910, working with fruit flies, T. H. Morgan showed that chromosomes carry the genes that determine an organism's traits.

HOW IT ALL WORKS

Genetics is a vast and complicated field. Even today, scientists are working to understand more about the details of how traits are passed from one organism to another. However, the basics of this complex branch of science were established years ago by hardworking, creative researchers.

DISCOVERING DNA

After learning how chromosomes carry genes, scientists worked to understand genes themselves. They soon discovered that genes work by controlling the creation of **enzymes** in a cell. Enzymes are **proteins** that control a cell's functions.

In the 1940s, scientists learned that genes are made of a substance called deoxyribonucleic acid (DNA). DNA is made up of sugar, a chemical called phosphate, and four other chemicals known as bases. These four bases are adenine (A), guanine (G), cytosine (C), and thymine (T). In DNA, two bases are always attached together. A always pairs with T. G always pairs with C. These pairs are strung together in long strands. The order of the bases in the chain acts as a sort of code for making different enzymes.

THE SHAPE OF THINGS TO COME

In 1953, scientists Francis Crick and James Watson discovered the shape of DNA strands. The base pairs are like steps on a twisting ladder. Sugar and phosphate form the sides of the ladder. The shape is called a double helix. Watson and Crick also showed that this shape allows strands of DNA to create copies of themselves when cells divide. This process transfers the information stored in genes into new cells.

DNA, RNA, AND ENZYMES

By the early 1970s, scientists had confirmed the importance of DNA in controlling heredity and shaping an organism's traits. Three bases in a row on a strand of DNA created the code for making substances called **amino acids**. The amino acids then formed the enzymes that controlled a cell's functions.

James Watson (left) and Francis Crick (right) pose with their DNA model in 1953.

LADDER SIDES FORMED FROM SUGAR AND PHOSPHATE

BASES PAIR TOGETHER

Discovering the structure of DNA was a major breakthrough in genetics.

Over the decades, scientists learned that a substance called ribonucleic acid (**RNA**) was also an important part of genetics. RNA transports the code for making enzymes from DNA to a part of the nucleus called the ribosome. The ribosome is where the enzymes are actually made. ※

Professor Stanley Cohen poses in his lab in Nashville, Tennessee, in 1986.

THE FIRST GENETIC ENGINEERING

In 1972, scientists Stanley Cohen and Herbert Boyer were thinking of ways to take genes from one organism and put them in another. Cohen was working with plasmids. These are parts of DNA in **bacteria** that are separate from the chromosomes. Boyer was studying a type of enzyme in bacteria that defends against invading organisms by attacking their genes.

Together, Cohen and Boyer realized they could use plasmids along with these enzymes to give bacteria new traits from other bacteria. The plasmid would carry the new genetic material, while the enzyme cut apart the existing gene so the new one could be added.

Cohen and Boyer also realized that the same process could transfer genes between entirely different organisms. They used it to insert genes from a toad into bacteria. The next generations of bacteria had the toad genes. With this discovery, genetic engineering was born.

PROTEIN FACTORIES

Because bacteria reproduce quickly, they were able to act as a "factory" for producing enzymes normally found in another species. All Boyer and Cohen had to do was give the bacteria genes from another organism that produced the desired protein. In 1976, Boyer worked with an investor to start a company to produce medicines this way. Over the next few years, scientists at the company produced several human proteins in bacteria. These included **insulin**, which is used as a medication for people who have diabetes. The bodies of people with diabetes don't produce enough insulin on their own.

In 1981, scientists created the first **transgenic** mammal that could pass on new traits to its children. Transgenic animals contain artificially introduced genes. Soon scientists were engineering mice by adding or taking away different genes. The mice were useful for researching the role of the genes in causing certain illnesses.

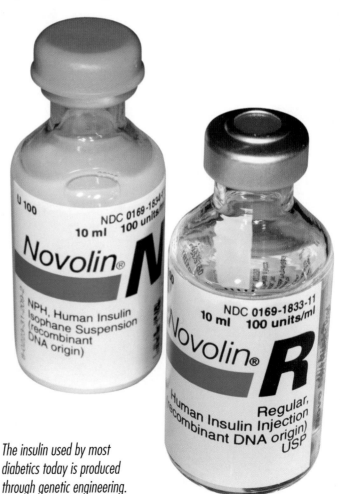

The insulin used by most diabetics today is produced through genetic engineering.

BARBARA MCCLINTOCK'S CORN

Genetics was still a new field when Barbara McClintock began studying it during the 1920s. McClintock combined her interest in genes with the study of plants to make many important discoveries. Most other scientists, however, did not recognize the importance of her work until decades later.

Corn kernels come in a wide variety of colors.

GENES ON THE MOVE

McClintock performed much of her research on corn. In the lab, she learned how to color the cells so she could pick out the plant's 10 distinct chromosomes. She also learned which genes are inherited together because they are on the same chromosome. On the farm, she grew plants that produced different colored kernels of corn and tracked how the patterns of colors changed over generations. Between her work in the lab and on the farm, McClintock discovered that genes can move within a chromosome and even between them. These genes were nicknamed jumping genes. Today they're known as transposons.

Barbara McClintock was eventually recognized for her work with the 1983 Nobel Prize in Physiology or Medicine.

A professor at Ohio State University examines tomatoes being used in genetic studies.

MOVEMENT AND MUTATIONS

Before McClintock's work, geneticists thought genes were strung out in a line on chromosomes and never moved. With the discovery of jumping genes, McClintock saw that where a gene moved could affect the behavior of other genes. She suggested that the moving genes did not pass on traits. Instead, they were genetic material that somehow controlled other genes. As they moved, they created **mutations** that disrupted genes around them.

TRANSPOSONS TODAY

Other scientists of the time mostly rejected McClintock's ideas. By the 1970s, however, biologists knew that transposons existed in many organisms. In humans, they make up about 65 percent of the **genome**, or all the DNA in the body.

Scientists now use transposons in genetic engineering. They can be used to add a genetic trait to an organism or to turn off an existing gene. During the 1990s, Israeli scientists used transposons to shut off genes that controlled a tomato plant's size and leaf color. The altered tomato plants were used in research to track gene mutations.

SEARCHING FOR SEQUENCES

In 1964, the U.S. biologist Robert Holley led a team that discovered the pattern of bases in yeast RNA, a process called sequencing. During the 1970s, Frederick Sanger and others did the same thing with DNA, which is more complex than RNA. Gene sequencing let scientists know the exact arrangement of a segment of DNA or RNA that was responsible for creating different genes. This made it easier to figure out how to alter, remove, or insert sequences to affect an organism's traits.

Sequencing has remained an important part of genetics. Today, scientists work to sequence the entire genomes of different species instead of just specific genes. The more they discover, the greater the possibilities for future advancements in genetic engineering.

BASES

A strand of RNA has a single helix shape, which makes it look like a DNA strand cut in half.

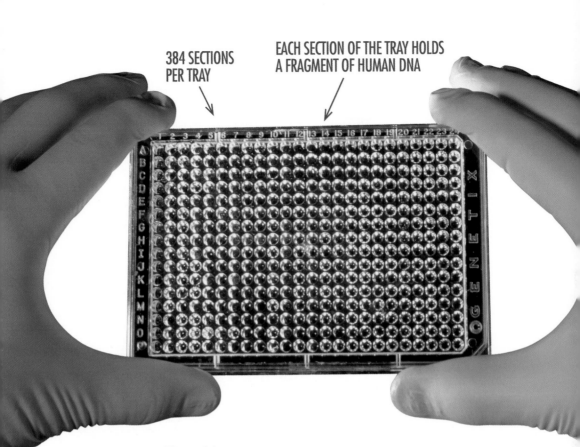

384 SECTIONS PER TRAY

EACH SECTION OF THE TRAY HOLDS A FRAGMENT OF HUMAN DNA

The human genome fills 60 of these trays.

NEW RESEARCH, NEW PRODUCTS

During the 1980s, scientists continued to alter the genes of many organisms. As a result of this work, the first genetically altered foods appeared in grocery stores in the 1990s. The first one to reach supermarket shelves was a tomato that stayed firm long after it was picked. Around the same time, genetic engineering yielded new medicines to treat certain kinds of cancer.

During the 1990s, scientists began to study the human genome. They had already mapped the genomes of other, smaller organisms. By 2003, scientists had a complete catalog of the human genome. This has made it easier to see which genes cause illnesses. With this information, scientists can create possible genetic treatments for the diseases.

By changing a plant's DNA, scientists can improve traits of the fruits and vegetables we eat everyday.

2

GENETIC ENGINEERING TODAY

I f you slice an apple and let a piece sit out, it soon turns brown. But what if you could alter the genes of an apple so it would stay fresh longer? That's how the Arctic apple was created. Scientists shut off a gene that controls the production of a protein that makes the apple turn brown.

Every year, countless potatoes are thrown away because they have been bruised. However, the Innate Russet Burbank potato variety is able to resist bruising, thanks to genetic modification.

All foods containing genetically modified organisms (GMOs) must be approved by the government before they can be sold in the United States. Both the Arctic apple and the Innate Russet Burbank potato were approved in 2015. They are just two of the many GMO foods scientists have created in recent years.

GMO FOOD HIGHLIGHTS

1994	1995	1998	2004	2008
The Flavr Savr tomato is created to stay fresh longer than standard tomatoes.	Corn is altered to help fight off insects.	A variety of papaya that can fight off a deadly disease is introduced.	Golden rice produces an important vitamin not found in white rice.	Sugar beets are altered to resist chemicals used to kill weeds.

Genetically modified foods are a common sight on grocery store shelves today.

CHANGING THE FOOD WE EAT

In many ways, genetic engineering is replacing traditional chemistry as the method of solving problems and creating new products. Genetic engineering can result in products that are cheaper and easier to make. It can also cut down on the amount of raw materials needed to make products. This makes many genetically engineered products more environmentally friendly than traditional versions.

For typical North Americans, genetic engineering may have its biggest impact on the foods they eat. Almost all the soybeans and corn grown in the United States are GMOs. These crops end up in a wide range of products sold in grocery stores, from cookies and chips to salad dressing.

Most GMO foods are altered to make them easier to grow in some way. Depending on what they grow, farmers can use fewer chemicals or grow more crops on smaller areas of land. Corn and soy are altered so the plants won't be killed by chemicals that kill weeds. Scientists have also made several crops able to fight off harmful insects.

CREATING CLONES

Crops aren't the only genetically engineered source of food. In Texas, some farmers are hoping to use cattle clones to produce a larger amount of quality meat. Cloning is a process that allows organisms to be created artificially using genetic material. To clone a cow, scientists take DNA from an animal that has desirable traits. Then they insert it into an egg cell from a female of the same species. The egg develops, and, if all goes well, a baby is born. The baby produced through this process is almost an exact copy of the animal that provided the DNA. Only a small amount of DNA comes from the original DNA of the egg cell. As a result, the clone has the traits of the source animal.

The first mammal cloned from the DNA of an adult animal was a sheep born in 1996. Since then, scientists have cloned horses, rabbits, cats, dogs, and other animals. One experiment that began in 2014 produced puppies cloned from a dog that was specially trained by the U.S. military. The scientists involved hoped the clones would easily develop the same skills as the source dog.

Clones such as Dolly the sheep look identical to animals born from natural reproductive methods.

FROM THIS TO THAT

DRILL DIGS UNDERGROUND TO ACCESS FOSSIL FUELS

Genetic research could help reduce our reliance on fossil fuels, which can be harmful to the environment.

FROM FOSSIL FUELS TO BIOFUELS

Planes, cars, and ships carry people all over the world. Huge computer servers store information that can be accessed from almost anywhere. Billions of people flick a switch, and lights go on in their homes. All these activities rely on a source of energy.

For several hundred years, people have used fossil fuels for much of their energy. These fuels are found on or beneath Earth's surface. They include coal, oil, and natural gas. But burning fossil fuels creates gases that harm the environment. In addition, these fuels will one day run out, and they can't be replaced.

One way to address the need for more and cleaner energy sources comes from genetic engineering. Scientists are exploring several different ways of modifying organisms so they can turn plants into an energy source for cars and homes. Fuel sources made from living things are often called biofuels.

Ethanol is a type of biofuel that is usually made from corn or sugar plants.

NEW FUELS FROM PLANTS

In 2013, scientists in California found a way to alter the genes in bacteria so they can turn more of the sugar in plants into energy. The new process will make it cheaper to produce biofuel from wood chips and grass.

Another gene modification reduces the production of lignin in plants. This chemical interferes with the process of turning plants into fuel. Plants need some lignin to grow, but with less of it, companies spend less money making biofuel.

ENERGY FROM ALGAE

Scientists have also modified algae to produce biofuel. Algae are single-celled organisms found in water. On their own, they can produce a form of oil almost like the kind used to make gasoline. With genetic engineering, algae can be changed to produce oil that can easily be turned into gas for cars. The method for making algae oil is still expensive, but it should become cheaper over time. ✳

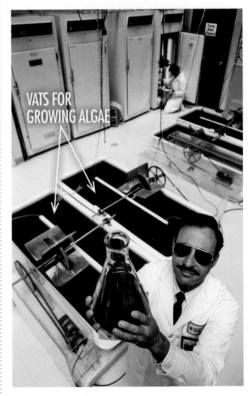

VATS FOR GROWING ALGAE

Scientist Lewis Brown shows off a flask full of oil-producing algae.

MAKING MEDICINE

Plants have also been altered so they can produce medicine, just as bacteria were during the 1970s. For example, genetically modified tobacco plants have produced medicines that fight a wide range of diseases. In 2014, scientists tested a treatment for Ebola that was developed this way.

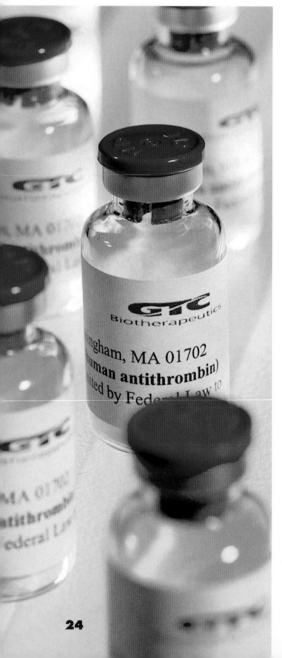

Mammals can be altered to produce medicines, too. In 2006, a drug called ATryn became the first useful medication made using transgenic animals. Some humans lack antithrombin, a protein that stops blood from forming clots in the body. Scientists took the gene that produces antithrombin and added it to goats. The altered goats then produced the protein in their milk. Scientists are working to create other medicines in a similar way.

ATryn was approved for use on human patients in 2009.

Many people prefer to avoid GMO foods whenever possible.

CONTROVERSY

Cloned mammals and GMO crops have raised concerns among the public. In some species, cloned animals seem more prone to certain diseases. They often die young. People who oppose cloning say the process is cruel to the animals that suffer after they're born. Some cloning opponents also worry that scientists might one day try to clone humans. They worry about the same health dangers animals face. They also fear that society would no longer see each person as truly unique if a copy can be made in a lab.

Some people worry that the safety of eating GMO crops is not truly known, even though the government requires testing before a GMO can be sold. For example, a person could be allergic to the source of the DNA added to a crop and have a bad reaction to it. Several U.S. states have called for clear labeling of GMO foods. This would help people avoid them if they choose. However, most scientists believe that GMOs are just as safe as traditional foods.

NATURALLY BORN
HOUSE CAT

CLONED WILDCAT

A cloned African wildcat kitten named Jazz was born from a house cat named Cayenne in 1999.

SAVING ANIMAL SPECIES

In Louisiana, scientists at the Audubon Center for Research of Endangered Species have been testing the idea of cloning endangered species. These scientists started by cloning an African wildcat. A regular house cat provided the egg cell and carried the embryo. In 2005, the center made history when cloned male and female wildcats produced offspring of their own. Though the process is experimental, cloning could one day be a way to save endangered animals from extinction.

Another method of genetic engineering may offer endangered species more hope. It is called facilitated adaptation. Scientists may facilitate, or help, species survive threats in their natural environments. Across the world, temperatures are rising. This climate change could make it hard for some species to survive where they now live. With facilitated adaptation, scientists would take genes from a related species that can live in warmer temperatures. The animals facing extinction would receive these genes, which could make it possible for them to adapt to higher temperatures.

BACK FROM THE DEAD

Genetic scientists are also discussing something called de-extinction. They wonder if a preserved cell from an extinct animal could be used as the source for a clone of that animal. The example scientists often discuss is the woolly mammoth, an ancestor of the elephant that lived long ago in cold climates.

Beth Shapiro is an expert in ancient DNA. She studies long-dead species by analyzing the DNA in their preserved bones. She believes that a true clone of the mammoth is unlikely because cloning requires a living cell. However, she sees a time when scientists might be able to change the DNA of an elephant to make it more like a woolly mammoth's. The change might make it easier for modern elephants to survive in colder areas. That way, African elephants facing extinction might survive elsewhere.

The fossilized bones of mammoths and other ancient animals still contain DNA after thousands or even millions of years.

MODERN MARVEL

The millions of visitors to the San Diego Zoo each year are unlikely to see the important genetic research going on behind the scenes.

THE FROZEN ZOO

The San Diego Zoo is one of the most famous zoos in the world. Countless visitors have enjoyed the zoo's incredible collection of animal species. But there's more to the zoo than just the animals on display. The Frozen Zoo is a facility at the San Diego Zoo that holds frozen cells taken from endangered or threatened animals. Scientists hope the genes inside these cells can be used to keep the species alive. The Frozen Zoo has cell samples from about 10,000 animals representing 1,000 species. It is the largest collection of its kind in the world.

LIQUID NITROGEN KEEPS SAMPLES FROZEN

THE WORK SO FAR

Using cells from the Frozen Zoo, scientists have produced clones of two endangered species. One is the gaur, or Indian bison, a member of the cow family that is found in parts of Asia. The other is the banteng, another wild cow found in Asia.

The Frozen Zoo also provided cells that were used to help sequence the genome of the black-footed ferret. Black-footed ferrets were almost extinct in the wild before zoos and the U.S. government began breeding them. Now, knowing

A researcher removes cell samples from a storage tank.

A scientist at the Frozen Zoo sequences DNA from horses and rhinoceroses.

the ferret's genome, scientists hope to study how genetic changes over time may have made it more difficult for the animal to survive in the wild. Their goal is to eventually alter the genes to help the ferret survive. ✳

The banteng is one of the many species scientists are trying to save through genetic engineering.

FROZEN ZOO

STORAGE TANKS CAN HOLD MANY SAMPLES

THE LATEST TECHNOLOGIES

Advances in genetic engineering are occurring all the time. A method that makes editing genes much easier, called CRISPR Cas9, was first described in 2012. The enzyme Cas9 follows the instructions of special RNA programmed by scientists to seek out certain segments of DNA. It then cuts out the desired strand.

Scientists see many possible uses for this technique. It makes all applications of genetic engineering much easier, faster, and cheaper. It could be used to treat genetic diseases. It could also be used to change the DNA in mosquitoes so they no longer transmit the disease malaria. Gene editing could be used to shut off genes and slowly wipe out the population of harmful animals that are accidentally transported around the world. These invasive species sometimes kill native species that humans want to keep alive.

In the future, mosquitoes could be genetically altered to not transmit malaria or other diseases.

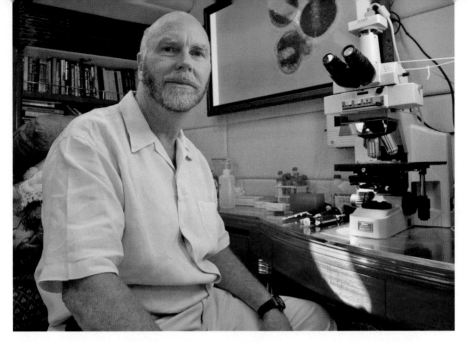

Dr. J. Craig Venter examines cells aboard a research ship.

CREATING LIFE FROM SCRATCH

Scientists have even used genetic engineering to create life in the lab. In 2010, a group of scientists made a copy of the genome of a small bacterium. They then assembled the chemicals of DNA in the right order and created a bacterium that lived and reproduced. Unlike cloning, they did not begin with the DNA of a bacterium that was already alive. They built the bacterium from scratch. The process took 15 years. The scientists hope they will be able to create bacteria that produce medicines or new sources of energy.

A GENOME PIONEER

J. Craig Venter wanted to be a medical doctor, but he ended up using his scientific skills for genetic research. Venter developed an easier way to identify genes, and his work during the 1990s helped map the human genome. He led the team that created the first genome of a living organism. Looking ahead, Venter thinks DNA sequences will one day be transmitted over the Internet and then be used to create organisms around the world.

DANDELION PLANTS

RUBBER MADE
FROM DANDELIONS

Scientists are searching
for ways to make products
from natural sources.

3

WORKING WITH GENES FOR A LIVING

W hen cars roll down the road, they ride on tires made of rubber. Some of this rubber is natural, from rubber trees. However, much of it comes from oil. Today, scientists are developing a new kind of rubber made from plants. They hope it will replace oil-based rubber.

Several companies have modified bacteria to turn the sugar in plants into rubber. Unlike traditional rubber, the plant-based version comes from a source that will never run out. Producing it does not hurt the environment.

Dandelions also produce a substance like the material in rubber trees. Scientists are now altering genes of the common weed so it will grow larger and be easier to pick. Dandelion farms may one day provide some of the rubber that now comes from trees grown in only a few countries.

NOBEL PRIZE-WINNING GENETIC SCIENTISTS

1933	1962	1980	1983	2006
T. H. Morgan, Nobel Prize in **Physiology** or Medicine	Francis Crick, James Watson, and Maurice Wilkins, Nobel Prize in Physiology or Medicine	Frederick Sanger and Walter Gilbert, Nobel Prize in Chemistry	Barbara McClintock, Nobel Prize in Physiology or Medicine	Andrew Fire and Craig Mello, Nobel Prize in Physiology or Medicine

Scientists share ideas and work together as they perform genetic research.

THE SCIENTISTS OF GENES AND DNA

It is no simple matter to come up with an idea about how to modify an organism, test and perfect that process, and then make a product. It often takes many years and the work of many highly skilled scientists and their assistants. Today, scientists at universities, in the government, and at private companies and organizations share ideas with each other to make biotechnology happen.

Some biotech scientists specialize in the study of genes and heredity. Others combine that knowledge with a background in chemistry or the study of **microorganisms**. Students interested in biotech may also study plants and animals, especially if they're interested in creating GMO foods or livestock.

FROM THE CLASSROOM TO A CAREER

No matter what field they study, scientists usually go through many years of college before starting their career. Most obtain a PhD, the highest university degree available. While pursuing their degrees, students conduct research alongside more experienced scientists. Scientists continue to learn even after they leave college. They have to keep up with the new discoveries made by other scientists in their fields.

Students who don't pursue advanced degrees in science can still find jobs in genetic engineering. They might assist others in research labs or use computers to process the information that other scientists discover.

The biotech industry also has a business side. Scientists who start their careers in the lab might end up selling genetically modified products to companies or even running companies of their own. Such jobs might require skills in finance, computers, or sales.

Biology and chemistry classes are an important part of a genetic scientist's education.

MEDICAL SCIENTISTS

Medical scientists try to find ways to cure diseases. They might work to develop traditional medicines or treatments that rely on genetic engineering. Most of these scientists have a PhD in a scientific field, and some are also medical doctors. Medical doctors who see patients instead of performing research in a lab might study genetic **pathology** as well. They learn how to use DNA and RNA testing to look for diseases.

As with many of the careers in genetic engineering, the exact tasks medical scientists do depend on where they work. Medical scientists at universities might take a broad view of what causes a disease and how it could be treated. At a biotech company, medical scientists might put more time into altering organisms that can produce a medicine the company can sell. Or they might alter viruses that can bring copies of healthy DNA into a patient's body.

Some genetic scientists spend most of their time performing experiments in a lab.

A cytogeneticist can offer useful information to parents about the health of their unborn children.

MOLECULAR GENETICISTS AND CYTOGENETICISTS

DNA and RNA are kinds of **molecules**. Molecular geneticists study the details of those molecules. With DNA, their goal is to determine exactly which genes control certain functions in an organism. They also try to learn how mutations in a gene might cause a disease. Molecular geneticists sometimes specialize in genes that are associated with disorders in particular parts of the body. A neurogeneticist, for example, might study genes that contribute to conditions such as autism. As in other scientific fields, a molecular geneticist might conduct research directly or supervise a staff carrying out the research.

Cytogeneticists focus on the study of chromosomes. For example, a pregnant woman might have the chromosomes of her unborn baby tested to see if the baby is likely to have a genetically triggered disease. Similar tests might be done on babies after they're born if they are not developing normally. The cytogeneticist can help determine if damaged chromosomes might be at fault.

Michael White has a PhD in biochemistry and is an Assistant Professor who researches genetics at the Washington University School of Medicine in St. Louis, Missouri. Here are some of his thoughts on the field of genetic engineering.

When did you start thinking about genetics as a career? What was it about the field that interested and inspired you? I started thinking about becoming a biologist in college. Before then I wanted to become a musician. In college I became interested in understanding how nonliving chemical parts like DNA and proteins work together to produce life.

What classes did you take to prepare for your career? I took basic classes in math, physics, chemistry, and biology in high school and college. Even though there are many different fields of biology, all biologists take classes in math, physics, chemistry, molecular biology, and genetics. Today, as computers play a bigger role in research, anyone interested in biology should also take classes in computer science and statistics.

What other projects and jobs did you do to prepare for what you do now? In college I studied music before turning to science, which helped because studying music helps you learn how to focus intensely. I need to focus in the same way when I solve a problem in science. After college, I also worked in the chemical lab at a factory, where I got to see how science is used to make actual products.

What are some of the specific academic paths that can lead to a job in your field? People become geneticists and genetic engineers in many different ways. Not all of them study biology in college—some study engineering, computer science, or physics instead, and then study biology later in their careers. No matter what you study in high school or college, the most important step is to train as a researcher in a genetics or biotechnology lab.

What kinds of jobs are in your field besides yours?

Geneticists work mostly at academic institutions or companies. At academic institutions, scientists focus on answering important scientific questions or developing new technologies. Scientists who work at companies are focused on taking basic scientific ideas or new technologies and developing them into a useful product that be sold.

Do you have a particular project that you're especially proud of?

One of my favorite projects was to use a new DNA technology to test how thousands of genes are controlled. In this experiment, I used both natural and engineered DNA to understand how our genes are switched on and off. I wasn't sure what the experiment would show, and it was exciting to see a surprising result that nobody had ever observed before.

It takes an entire team to do research or create a new product. Does working as a team come naturally for you, or was it something you had to learn and work on?

I like working as a team, because you get to try out your ideas with other people, and they share their new ideas with you. To me it comes naturally when you work with a good team. Actually making a new genetically modified product that is sold to customers requires people who make the business decisions, who decide if this is a good financial investment.

What would your dream job be if you were given unlimited resources?

I would like to run a research lab were I can study anything that I am curious about. With unlimited resources, we could try out challenging new ideas or solve difficult technological problems that would change the world if they worked, even if these projects took many years to complete.

What advice would you give a young person who wants to pursue a career in biotech/genetic engineering?

An important decision is to decide whether to get a PhD. If you like working in the lab instead of writing research reports and project proposals, then you can start working right after college. If you choose to get a PhD, it takes much longer before you really start your career. But this is the best way to gain the skills you need to invent new technologies and design new genetically engineered products. ✳

A scientist for the Monsanto Company cares for genetically modified tomato plants.

GENETIC ENGINEERS

This job title of "genetic engineer" is used by scientists with educational backgrounds in many different fields, such as biochemistry, cell biology, and molecular biology. Genetic engineers are usually employed by companies that make GMOs and other biotech products. They are involved in removing or adding sequences of DNA to organisms. They might step into the process after a molecular geneticist or some other scientist has already done the basic research to discover what a gene controls. Genetic engineers add the genes to plants that help them resist disease or alter the genes of a virus so it can deliver medicine to the human body. They might also help in keeping alive the microorganisms and cells that are part of their work.

COMPARATIVE GENETICISTS

While some scientists focus on the genome of one species, comparative geneticists work with the genes of several different organisms. They look to see how the genes of different species differ and how they're the same. Studying the genome of a closely related species such as a chimpanzee could help explain how similar genes work in humans. Scientists working in this field also study how genes have changed over time within a particular species as well as the similarities and differences of genes in related species.

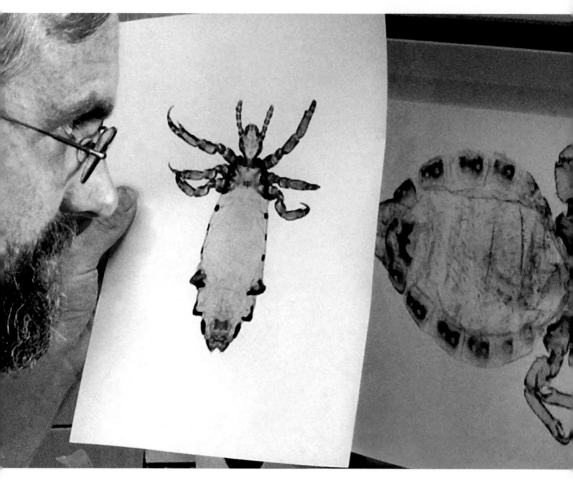

A researcher compares the genes of lice to learn about the different species these creatures feed on.

THE ARTISTIC SIDE

Watson and Crick built their DNA model using metal plates and rods.

THE BEAUTY OF DNA

The labs where scientists explore genetic engineering are not generally known for artwork. But decades ago, Francis Crick and James Watson were almost like sculptors as they created their model of DNA. They constructed the double helix model out of brass plates, steel, and objects around their lab. When they were done, the model was taller than they were. While no one called it a sculpture, Watson could only admire the beauty of the DNA's curves. A model of it is now on display at London's Science Museum.

DNA ORIGAMI

Scientists have also folded DNA into different shapes that can be viewed under a microscope. The process has been compared to origami, a traditional Japanese paper-folding art. Using DNA origami, scientists have made such shapes as smiley faces and snowflakes. But beyond making microscopic art, scientists could one day find useful purposes for DNA origami. For example, they could fold the DNA to make objects or parts of a tiny machine that could carry medicine into the body.

DNA11 creates custom artwork for clients who want to hang their own genetic codes on the wall.

YOUR DNA ON THE WALL

A Canadian company called DNA11 creates unique art based on its customers' DNA. One of the company's founders had an interest in genetics. The other was an artist. DNA11 extracts DNA from a sample of saliva and then processes it to reveal the customers' unique genetic code. Customers can then choose the colors they want in the art and how it will be framed. DNA11 built its own lab to turn the DNA into art. It is the first lab in the world to combine art and science in this way. ✳

In 2015, sculptures inspired by Crick and Watson's DNA model were placed throughout London, England, to raise awareness of genetic research.

FORENSIC DNA ANALYSTS

Forensic scientists in general use their skills to help solve crimes or otherwise settle legal issues. Within the field, DNA analysts specialize in collecting DNA evidence from victims and suspects and use it in police investigations and court cases. For example, if the DNA from a suspected murderer does not match the DNA found at a crime scene, the analyst can argue that the person was not involved with the murder. The research and development done by other biotechnology scientists give DNA analysts new tools for more accurately identifying DNA.

A forensic scientist studies bloodstained clothing as part of a criminal investigation.

A genetic counselor might have to deliver bad news to patients about their genetics.

BIOTECHNOLOGY JOBS AND PEOPLE

Some people in the biotech field have more direct contact with the public. These include clinical ethicists and genetic counselors. Ethics is the study of what is right and wrong behavior, apart from whether it is legal or not. Ethicists work with companies and governments to determine if a genetically modified process or product is ethical. For example, some people have questions about the ethics of scientists altering the genes of people or other organisms.

Genetic counselors work with people who carry genes that could pass on diseases to their children. They help the patients understand the risks of having children or offer support to people who have learned they have a disease caused by their genes.

White blood cells help protect the body from diseases.

FROM THE LAB TO YOU

C ancer is one of the deadliest illnesses in the world. It isn't just a simple disease with an obvious cause. It occurs when various causes, including genes, make certain cells grow more rapidly than normal and threaten the healthy cells around them.

Scientists are always looking for genetic medicines and techniques to fight cancer. The National Cancer Institute, for example, has spent several years working on a treatment to stop kidney cancer from spreading. Scientists use white blood cells from a patient to grow more of them in a lab. They then add a virus to the cells. The virus has been modified with a gene that shuts off the protein that helps cancer cells grow. The white blood cells with the modified virus inside are then returned to the patient's body. The hope is that the patient's body will produce more of the cancer-killing protein.

GENETICALLY ENGINEERED MEDICAL TREATMENTS

1978	1984	1992	2006	2010
Human insulin	Vaccine for hepatitis B	Blood-clotting protein	Vaccine to fight a virus that causes warts and a form of cancer	Treatment for prostate cancer

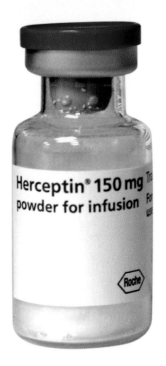

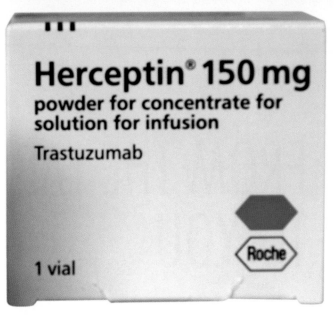

Herceptin is one of the many cancer drugs used today that is based on the discoveries of genetic researchers.

FIGHTING CANCER WITH GENES

The process of developing a new medical treatment can take years and the work of many different scientists. Here's a closer look at how one cancer drug, Herceptin, moved from the lab to hospitals, where it helps patients fight breast cancer.

Starting in the late 1970s, the company Genentech led the way in using genetic engineering to make medicines. Its research scientists learned that certain genes controlled cell growth. This knowledge interested oncologists—doctors who specialize in treating cancer—because cancer is a disease where cell growth is out of control. The oncologists wanted to learn if some of these genes might affect the growth of cells that cause breast cancer. Together, the doctors and the Genentech scientists pinpointed one gene that was associated with the cancer. Known as HER2, it was linked to some of the deadliest breast cancer cases. Patients who had more of the gene than normal were especially at risk.

DEVELOPING A NEW DRUG

The scientists' next step was to try to develop a medicine that could limit the effect of HER2 and try to stop the spread of breast cancer after it developed. Genetic engineers altered the genetics of mice to create proteins similar to ones that appear naturally in the human body. The proteins were **antibodies** designed to fight bacteria and viruses that cause illnesses. The manufactured antibodies would stop HER2's ability to make breast cancer cells grow. But before giving the mouse antibodies to a human, the scientists had to alter them. They combined the mouse antibodies with human antibodies so a patient's body would not reject the mouse protein as a foreign substance.

All this work did not guarantee that the new antibody would be tested. As a private company, Genentech wanted to make money, and testing is an expensive process. Some of the company's leaders did not want to spend money developing a new drug that might not work. But the scientists and oncologists insisted that it was worth at least testing the drug. The company finally agreed.

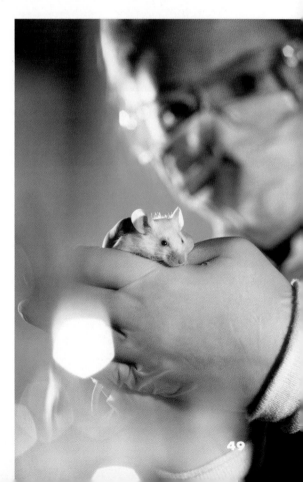

Mice are often used in genetic research because their genes are fairly similar to those of humans.

49

Genentech's headquarters is located in San Francisco, California.

MAKING MEDICINE IN CELLS

When someone has diabetes, his or her body produces little or no insulin. This protein helps control how the body processes the sugar found in different foods. Many people with diabetes need to inject insulin from another source to make their bodies function properly. The body normally produces insulin in an organ called the pancreas. The first insulin used as a medicine came from the pancreas of cows. But the development of genetic engineering led to a new source of insulin—humans.

RECOMBINANT DNA AND MEDICINE

When Stanley Cohen and Herbert Boyer first combined DNA from different organisms, the new DNA was called recombinant DNA. Boyer then went on to found Genentech. In 1978, the company created recombinant DNA insulin. Its scientists took the human genes for insulin and put them into bacteria. Inside the bacteria, insulin molecules were formed.

RECOMBINANT DNA MEDICINE TODAY

Today, a number of medicines are produced using recombinant DNA. These include drugs called interferons, which fight viruses, and a drug used to fight blood clots. Some interferons are produced in bacteria, as insulin is. Other times, the drugs are made in cells taken from animals. Whatever the source, recombinant DNA medicines play an important role in keeping people healthy. ✴

At one time, most insulin used to treat diabetes was produced using cows.

Herbert Boyer is one of the most influential scientists in the history of genetics.

Genentech's work marked the first time scientists had used recombinant DNA to create a medicine. In 1982, the government approved the use of lab-created human insulin to treat diabetes. The insulin could be produced faster and cheaper than insulin from cows or pigs. Since it came from humans and not animals, patients were less likely to have an allergic reaction to it.

TIME FOR TESTING

Before they can be sold as legal treatments, all potential medicines must be tested on human volunteers to ensure they work properly without harming patients. Generally, these volunteers have few other options for treatment. They are willing to risk the possibility of a negative side effect in order to find a cure. This testing process is called a clinical trial. The U.S. government has strict rules for how a trial is run. The first phase uses a small number of volunteers who have the disease the new medicine is designed to treat. This phase alerts doctors to possible harmful effects and helps them determine a safe dose for the drug. The next two phases add more volunteers each time. The doctors, nurses, and other health care workers involved in the trials observe the volunteers carefully to see how the medication is affecting them.

During a clinical study, doctors stay in close contact with patients to observe how the medication is working.

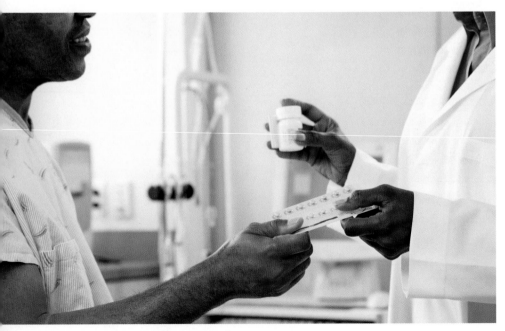

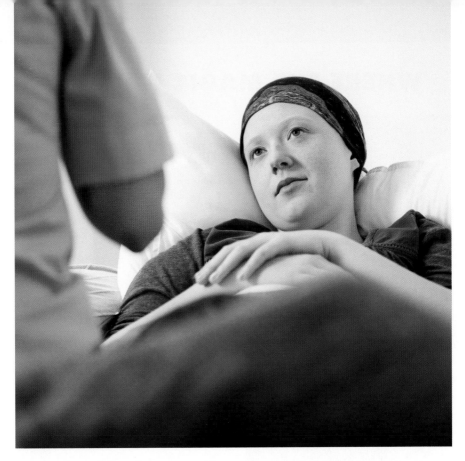

Cancer patients with few other options are often willing to try an experimental new treatment.

A LENGTHY PROCESS

In 1992, the oncologists at Genentech began trials on their medicine, which was later named Herceptin. To recruit more volunteers, Genentech contacted people who had breast cancer and no other treatment options. It also built a new plant to make more of the antibody. Over seven years, almost 1,000 breast cancer patients were given Herceptin to see if it could stop their illness from spreading.

A problem emerged during the third and final phase. Patients who took Herceptin along with another drug to fight their cancer had a high risk of heart problems. During the trial, the doctors learned that the risk was lower when Herceptin was not used along with that particular cancer drug.

WHERE THE MAGIC HAPPENS

Scientists Max Delbruck and Salvador Luria conduct genetics research at Cold Spring Harbor in 1941.

A LONG HISTORY OF SUCCESS

In 1900, several scientists discovered the work that Gregor Mendel had done decades before on heredity and genes. This sparked a new interest in genetics, and a New York school that taught biology to high school teachers became a center of genetics research. That school is known today as the Cold Spring Harbor Laboratory. It remains one of the world's most important centers of genetic studies.

MICE, CORN, AND MORE

During the 1910s and 1920s, Cold Spring Harbor researchers learned more about the connection between genes and cancer in mice. In 1940, Barbara McClintock came to Cold Spring Harbor to continue her work on the chromosomes of corn. During World War II, work done at the laboratory helped increase the production of the medicine penicillin, which can cure a wide range of diseases caused by bacteria.

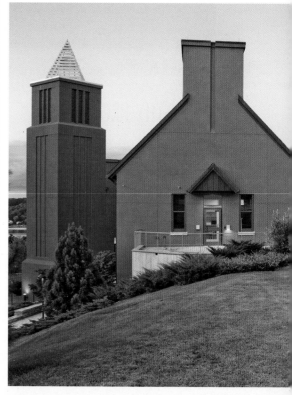

THE WORK CONTINUES

The discovery that genes were made of DNA, as well as the discovery of the structure of DNA, led to the modern era of genetic engineering. James Watson, who helped create the double helix model of DNA, came to Cold Spring Harbor in 1968. In the decades that followed, Cold Spring Harbor focused its research on cancer, neuroscience, and genetics. Today, studying the role of genes in causing

Cold Spring Harbor Laboratory is located on Long Island, New York.

Barbara McClintock conducts her research on corn genetics at Cold Spring Harbor.

cancer and other diseases is just one focus of the Cold Spring Harbor scientists. One area they explore is epigenetics, which looks at how factors in the environment can change genes without mutating them. For example, what people eat or which medicines they use may affect their genes. Cold Spring Harbor scientists also study the role of RNA in causing cancer. ✳

Many patients were relieved to see improvement in their condition after using Herceptin.

ONE THING LEADS TO ANOTHER

When combined with other drugs, Herceptin proved so useful that the U.S. government named it a "fast track" medicine. That means the Food and Drug Administration worked with Genentech to speed up the approval process. Further research since 1998 has shown that Herceptin can also help treat some stomach cancers that are linked to the HER2 gene. Since then, scientists have developed several more drugs to treat cancers linked to HER2.

Creating Herceptin helped some cancer patients, but Genentech researchers were not finished. They continued to study the role of HER2 in the spread of breast cancer. That led to the discovery of a second genetically engineered drug, Perjeta. Combined with Herceptin, it helped more cancer patients live longer.

MAKING MEDICINE PERSONAL

Herceptin is an example of what is now called a personalized medicine. Doctors seek to tailor their treatment to each patient. The idea is not new, but breakthroughs in genetic engineering have made this kind of treatment easier than ever. Only people who have a gene connected to the disease receive the genetically engineered medicine.

Professor David Lane was knighted by the British government in 2000 for his accomplishments in cancer research.

DAVID LANE

As a college student in England, David Lane watched his father die of cancer. This experience convinced the budding scientist to learn more about the disease and how it might be cured. As he started his career, Lane focused on viruses and how they affect the body. In 1979, this work led him to discover the gene P53. Lane's research showed that the gene played a role in controlling how cells grow. When P53 works as it should, cells grow normally and don't become cancerous. But a mutation in the gene can lead to cancer. Lane has continued to study P53 and has led other scientists to search for gene therapies that target it. The goal is to find treatments that can make the gene work properly, reducing the risk of cancer.

THE FUTURE

Genetic modifications make it possible to grow more crops using less space.

In the decades to come, interest in the role of genetics in human health will only grow. Scientists hope to discover more genes that cause disease and to engineer drugs that fight the genes' effect. Genetic engineering will also play a role in discovering diseases that are difficult to detect. Right now, tests are emerging to detect the DNA that different cancer cells release into the blood. These tests mean doctors don't have to perform surgery to get samples of cells that might be cancerous. They just need blood samples.

FEEDING THE WORLD

Genetic engineering is about much more than just medicine. In food production, more GMO crops designed to resist disease and pests will appear in the future. GMOs will also help address one of the world's biggest problems: how to provide enough nutritious food to the world's growing population. Some scientists are looking at using genetically modified yeast to produce a drink that tastes like cow's milk. The new product would reduce the use of resources needed to raise cows.

Genetic research could have a big effect on the milk we drink.

INCREASING SUSTAINABILITY

Reducing the amount of natural resources people use will be a focus for biotechnology in many fields. The world's growing population needs fuel as well as food. As the work with algae oil shows, genetic engineering may provide some of the resources the world needs. As the population grows and people use more natural resources, more organisms may be altered to produce goods.

DNA FINGERPRINTS

New research may help forensic scientists as well. The organisms living in each person's stomach and entire body are specific to that person. Samples of those organisms' DNA could be used to identify someone, just as fingerprints and human DNA do today. The next generation of genetic engineers and scientists will uncover many uses for the genes that control almost all life on Earth. ☀

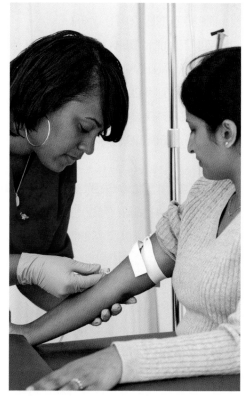

A simple blood sample could one day be used to diagnose diseases that are very hard to detect today.

CAREER STATS

BIOCHEMISTS, BIOPHYSICISTS, AND GENETICISTS

MEDIAN ANNUAL SALARY (2012): $81,480

NUMBER OF JOBS (2012): 29,200

PROJECTED JOB GROWTH (2012–2022): 19%, faster than average

PROJECTED INCREASE IN JOBS (2012–2022): 5,400

REQUIRED EDUCATION: At least a bachelor's degree; research scientists usually have doctorate degrees

LICENSE/CERTIFICATION: None

BIOMEDICAL ENGINEERS (INCLUDES GENETIC ENGINEERS)

MEDIAN ANNUAL SALARY (2012): $86,960

NUMBER OF JOBS (2012): 19,400

PROJECTED JOB GROWTH (2012–2022): 27%, much faster than average

PROJECTED INCREASE IN JOBS (2012–2022): 5,200

REQUIRED EDUCATION: At least a bachelor's degree; research scientists need advanced degrees, and some also become medical doctors

LICENSE/CERTIFICATION: State licensing required if serving as a medical doctor

MICROBIOLOGISTS (INCLUDES MOLECULAR BIOLOGISTS)

MEDIAN ANNUAL SALARY (2012): $66,260

NUMBER OF JOBS (2012): 20,100

PROJECTED JOB GROWTH (2012–2022): 7%, slower than average

PROJECTED INCREASE IN JOBS (2012–2022): 1,400

REQUIRED EDUCATION: At least a bachelor's degree; research scientists usually have doctorate degrees

LICENSE/CERTIFICATION: Usually only required for clinical microbiologists

Figures reported by the United States Bureau of Labor Statistics

RESOURCES

BOOKS

Bortz, Fred. *The Laws of Genetics and Gregor Mendel*. New York: Rosen Publishing, 2014.

Brinkerhoff, Shirley. *Research Scientist*. Broomall, PA: Mason Crest, 2014.

Einspruch, Andrew. *DNA Detectives*. New York: PowerKids Press, 2013.

Hicks, Terry Allan. *The Pros and Cons of Biofuel*. New York: Cavendish Square, 2015.

Spangenburg, Ray, and Diane Moser. *Barbara McClintock: Pioneering Geneticist*. New York: Chelsea House Publishers, 2008.

Szumski, Bonnie. *Careers in Biotechnology*. San Diego: ReferencePoint Press, 2015.

Thompson, Tamara. *Genetically Modified Food*. Farmington Hills, MI: Greenhaven Press, 2014.

FACTS FOR NOW

Visit this Scholastic Web site for more information on genetic engineering:
www.factsfornow.scholastic.com
Enter the keywords **Genetic Engineering**

GLOSSARY

amino acids (uh-MEE-no AS-idz) substances that serve as the building blocks of proteins

antibodies (AN-ti-bah-deez) proteins made by white blood cells to fight off invading microorganisms, such as bacteria

bacteria (bak-TEER-ee-uh) tiny living creatures that can be both helpful and harmful to people

chromosomes (KROH-muh-sohmz) long strands of DNA that contain genes

DNA (DEE EN AYE) the molecule that carries our genes, found inside the nucleus of cells; DNA is short for deoxyribonucleic acid

embryo (EM-bree-oh) the first development of a plant or animal

enzymes (EN-zymz) proteins that cause chemical changes in an organism

genes (JEENZ) the parts that make up chromosomes; genes are passed from parents to children and determine how you look and the way you grow

genome (JEE-nohm) the complete set of DNA in a living thing

heredity (huh-RED-i-tee) the process of passing traits from one generation of an organism to the next

insulin (IN-suh-lin) a hormone produced in the pancreas that regulates the level of sugar in the blood

microorganisms (mye-kroh-OR-guh-niz-uhmz) living creatures too small to be seen without a microscope

molecules (MAH-luh-kyoolz) chemicals made up of more than one atom

mutations (myoo-TAY-shuhnz) changes, often harmful, in a gene

organisms (OR-guh-niz-uhmz) living things, such as plants or animals

pathology (puh-THAH-luh-gee) the study of the causes of disease

physiology (fi-zee-AH-luh-gee) the study of how the parts of living organisms function

proteins (PROH-teenz) chemical compounds found in all living cells

RNA (AR EN AYE) the complex molecule produced by living things and viruses that is responsible for manufacturing the protein in a cell; RNA is short for ribonucleic acid

transgenic (trans-JEH-nik) an organism containing artificially introduced genes

INDEX

Page numbers in *italics* indicate illustrations.

INDEX *(CONTINUED)*

ABOUT THE AUTHOR

MICHAEL BURGAN is the author of more than 250 books for children and young adults, both fiction and nonfiction. His books on science include *Developing Flu Vaccines, Not a Drop to Drink: Water for a Thirsty World,* and biographies of several scientists and inventors. A graduate of the University of Connecticut with a degree in history, Burgan is also a produced playwright and the editor of *The Biographer's Craft.* He lives in Santa Fe, New Mexico.